A SEASON IN HELL WITH RIMBAUD

A SEASON IN HELL WITH RIMBAUD

POEMS

DUSTIN PEARSON

AMERICAN POETS CONTINUUM SERIES, NO. 193

BOA EDITIONS, LTD. ◉ ROCHESTER, NY ◉ 2022

First Edition
22 23 24 25 7 6 5 4 3 2 1

For information about permission to reuse any material from this book, please contact The Permissions Company at www.permissionscompany.com or e-mail permdude@ gmail.com.

Publications by BOA Editions, Ltd.—a not-for-profit corporation under section 501 (c) (3) of the United States Internal Revenue Code—are made possible with funds from a variety of sources, including public funds from the Literature Program of the National Endowment for the Arts; the New York State Council on the Arts, a state agency; and the County of Monroe, NY. Private funding sources include the Max and Marian Farash Charitable Foundation; the Mary S. Mulligan Charitable Trust; the Rochester Area Community Foundation; the Ames-Amzalak Memorial Trust in memory of Henry Ames, Semon Amzalak, and Dan Amzalak; the LGBT Fund of Greater Rochester; and contributions from many individuals nationwide. See Colophon on page 96 for special individual acknowledgments.

NATIONAL
ENDOWMENT
for the ARTS
arts.gov

State of the Arts

NYSCA

Cover Design: Sandy Knight
Cover and Interior Art: Nathan Mullins
Interior Composition: Richard Foerster
BOA Logo: Mirko

BOA Editions books are available electronically through BookShare, an online distributor offering Large-Print, Braille, Multimedia Audio Book, and Dyslexic formats, as well as through e-readers that feature text to speech capabilities.

Library of Congress Cataloging-in-Publication Data

Names: Pearson, Dustin, author.
Title: A season in Hell with Rimbaud : poems / Dustin Pearson.
Description: First edition. | Rochester, NY : BOA Editions, Ltd., 2022. |
    Series: American poets continuum series ; 193 | Summary: "In pursuit of his
    brother, a man traverses the fantastical and grotesque landscape of Hell, pondering
    their now fractured relationship"— Provided by publisher.
Identifiers: LCCN 2021042524 (print) | LCCN 2021042525 (ebook) | ISBN
    9781950774593 (paperback) | ISBN 9781950774609 (epub)
Subjects: LCGFT: Poetry.
Classification: LCC PS3616.E25436 S43 2022 (print) | LCC PS3616.E25436
    (ebook) | DDC 811/.6—dc23
LC record available at https://lccn.loc.gov/2021042524
LC ebook record available at https://lccn.loc.gov/2021042525

BOA Editions, Ltd.
250 North Goodman Street, Suite 306
Rochester, NY 14607
www.boaeditions.org
A. Poulin, Jr., Founder (1938–1996)

for Pree and for poets with no guarantees

Contents

IV

V

VI

◙   ◙   ◙

A Season in Hell with Rimbaud

I dreamt I was showing my brother around in Hell.
We started inside the house.
Everything was brown besides the white sheets
in the bedrooms. I let him look
outside the window, told him it was hottest there,
where the flames rolled against the glass,
as if a giant mouth were blowing them,
as if there were thousands caught in the storm,
pushing it onward with mindless running,
save a desperation for something else.
How had there been a house in Hell
and we invited with time to spend? Why was it
I hadn't questioned how I got there? My brother
growing so tired from the heat, the sweating?
Surely we could open the door, he said. *Surely there'll be*
a breeze. Even seeing already, even burning himself
on the doorknob. His eyes turned back in his head
working his way to the bedrooms, staining
the sheets with his blistered hands, and though I knew the beds
weren't for the rest of any body, I sat by and let him sleep.

Regardless,

Hell is a state of mind I slipped into
years ago, tossing a red balloon
to my brother. Even then,

       I'd never be able to do what he couldn't.
       I'd always fall short of what he could do.
       I couldn't convince myself

I went because I loved him. His descent
would show me where mine ended. We'd be
together this way if it was the last thing

       we wanted, but he'd pave the path
       as nature intended. Our house in Hell
       was right under the one we lived in

with our parents. The stairs unearthed
a black spiral sharper than glass.
Sweat loosed from our pores on the trek

       down, shrunk our skin to its hardest wrap
       on our muscles, and made the stairs slick,
       daring us to fall or take an endless trip

with equal risk. Every cut on our feet
bled, and the blood that leaked
formed puddles under us that mixed.

       There were times we walked
       side by side, at others I walked
       in front or behind, but that first time

I lost my balance, I was devastated, not knowing
why he grabbed my hand. Why he held it
from that point forward. Why he hadn't

       accepted like I did, that regardless
       of how we got to the bottom,
       we'd see each other again.

Watching My Brother Sleep in Hell,
a Memory Reminds Me This Too Is Bonding

Having burned himself so badly,
it was a wonder he'd managed
to get in bed, or more, fall asleep.
Pulling the sheets from the headboard,
his hands wet them with pus
and bleeding, his blistered fingers
curling a grip and weak crinkling
on the silk threads. It wasn't until I went
to college, had been entrusted to look after
dorm residents, that I knew how especially
like me it is to see a wound and soothe it.
With my brother, the instinct was timid.
Watching over him, I remembered
the bloody, scabbed-over craters, the
unpopped domes of infection to be
blown open on this one resident.
He'd made a habit of sitting shirtless
in seats, in front of his computer,
and at night the wounds would leak
yellow-green and red into his bedding,
crust over a bit and streak on his skin
in his toss-turn dreaming. I asked if
I could help him, brushed four medicines
inside each of the holes he ripped
into himself. He said we'd been bonding,
me doing the thing on him with the medicine,
and he sitting. I'd have said
I was treating the acne he couldn't see,
but I'm sure the creams, my spreading of them,
felt cool on him, their gentle-clean, numbing,
mint-like aromatics, and that moment,
and those reliefs, he associated with me.

The next morning, I had a look at him,
asking if my treatment worked before
he turned to show me. The holes shrunk,
and the redness around them lessened.
I never did as much for my own brother.
My brother had a better back, but when
we were young, we did something similar.
Sometimes when one of us got a bump
that itched, the other would rub it.
The adults around us warned scratching
would lead to infection, so we decided
infection wouldn't happen left to the other's hand,
less apt to destruction on another body,
and more patient. I remember
I had a ringworm on the underside
of my forearm. My brother made
small circles around it with his middle finger.
I sat quiet and still, that ringworm
had made me restless, but while
my brother was there, I had peace.
After a while, he predicted the pus that would
come out of it. When he stopped to show me,
a clear liquid started bubbling up to the point
I could see. Had the pus touched the underside
of his finger, made it wet in a way
he could recognize? Had the worm somehow
changed in texture? Softened? Those things
were so contagious. We entered in careless.

My Brother Outside the House in Hell

I fell asleep after I told myself I'd watch him.
What convinced him
there was relief to find
in the flames outside
when he'd seen already
what I showed him?
I woke to his smell.
The heat of the door
and his turning of its knob
burned to the bone before
he could get it open.
His flesh fell uneven
and beaded on the hardwood.
The circling flames
blew through. A plume
of hellfire brushed me back
from where I'd been standing,
but I rushed
to the one window
to track him. I watched
my brother running, the flames
in a cruel attachment
to his skin, his arms
flailing. He ran
with his mouth open,
screaming,
as everyone outside was,
and crying, though
no tears, no
intimate evidence
of conditions. The fire
took his face,
and for his skull,

all I could think was
how we'd once been told
that deep down
the two of us were identical,
beyond the arrangement
of muscle and its appearance.
I knew the house
would never let my brother
back in, but even waking
from the dream, I knew
I wouldn't wake
from any decision
to leave us separated,
leaving everything
in the moment
our eyes opened
to unite us, but even
migrating to the door,
I couldn't open it.
Between burns
on my hands and anticipating
the pain of the outside,
I failed each time.
I walked back
to the window, watched
my brother disappear.
I was left alone in the house,
my brother finally
let to roam. And though
I knew under those terms
we'd never see each other again,
I knew we found a home
outside the sea
of each other.

A Dependency

You can lose your brother to Hell
and still be happy inside your house.
The house has many rooms. You find
elegance in its brown walls and furnishings,
and though the flames that rush past
the window make everything bright inside
with the dozens of doors closed,
you can streak all over and no one
will ever see you. If you had neighbors,
you'd bring out your brown china and crystal,
and bourbon you'd pair with browned
hors d'oeuvres. You'd invite them
over to see your view of the fires
even as they're envious enough to break in.
You don't get used to the heat, but you were
born in a hot place, so you tell yourself
you're suited to rising temperatures.
You never understood the white sheets
of the bedrooms, why your brother
had opted to sleep. It takes hours,
but you manage to fall asleep, being
so still that your dreams take you away
to a mountaintop, a world of greens
and violent and churning blues. In
your house in Hell, there's a nightstand,
a white picket fence around a porch.
You meet a girl, a brown lamp
with a brown shade, and every moment
of happiness in the house with your eyes open
is one you realize your brother is missing.

The Day I Told My Brother That Despite It All, I Found a Way to Be Happy

I remember bursting through the door
to tell my brother the good news, half confident
it wouldn't bring about conflict because

this happiness I found would never look like his.
If I could prove it hadn't come from the source
he drew from, I could be happy

without taking away from him.
There were things in the world
we could share if they weren't his,

but I was petrified, not knowing
whether he'd embrace me or be jealous,
if I could make a difference.

It had been years since I'd
been embraced. I wanted to tell,
but for how happy I'd been, I buried it,

that twinkling veiled to a point
I could hardly stand, and where
the light leaked, he could see,

and with each look he gave me,
the sadness imposed darkening.
I remember how the dark seeped

when night fell on the house, the way
it collected in the hall, on the stairs
separating my room from his

after the drapes had been drawn.
I remember thinking there was enough
buried light for the path to each other

to never be dangerous if only for knowing
the monster the light would bring
wouldn't be either of us. There's no need

to bring light to Hell. All its monsters
are illuminated by flames and in that way,
everything is open, but even here,

there are those who go missing. It wasn't long ago
a woman got buried. She'd wandered off weeping
and got trapped under Hell's falling debris.

No number of us could recover her. Her screams
were two-fold under grief and burning,
and even if only weathering Hell

could make that state fall short of forever,
she had at least as much hope as I did
for my brother, for me.

Things I've Thought, Things I Do

Your brother is as strong as an ox. There were always people telling me that. I think maybe because I was short, still taller than he was, and skinny, or at least it seemed because of the clothes I wore. His body was bulky, no fat to be seen, and everyone stood in awe of its feats.

◎

Without breaking, he could clap a boulder to dust, but I didn't mind being invisible for being a mystery, didn't mind receiving the intel as a kind of disbelief. They were unwilling to look at both of our faces.

◎

Without heroics, what strength does it take to walk willingly, for one's mind to be so clouded by other pains, fire becomes a best rescue?

◎

I don't like to, but when I think about it, my brother and I had done the same thing. He walked out of our house into Hell's engulfing to get away from voices he couldn't quell, but being the only one left in the house, the only thing I could see he got away from was me.

◎

Had I listened to the people my brother shared his life with, the people volunteering to tell me who he was, I might've believed Hell couldn't ravage my brother's body.

◎

Brother, who in your life would you walk through fire for?

The thought of asking that question used to bother me, having to listen to a list that didn't include me,

or thinking the one name you'd say wouldn't be mine.

If you asked me, I don't think anyone would come to mind, at least not anyone on the outside. I considered that a failure in my life. Where we stood was already burning.

◎

Brother, I never thought my answer would be you. I'm not disappointed like I thought I'd be.

Pain on a Soft Surface

The wind in Hell is a scorch screen of momentum.
You hope there's a mouth you can crawl in,
a soft surface or cavity that could hold you
from it. There were thousands of bodies running,
but granted a reprieve from the crowd,
I always walked. My brother had gone off
sooner into the storm and had always been
a faster runner, arms flailing with wildness,
fully extended from his shoulders. I told myself
there was hope in the disparity of our paces.
He was the first person who told me I stood out,
something my mother had tried to, lovingly,
make me feel, something my father denied
completely. I resigned myself to the idea.
In a man's world, I'd never be anything,
even if I'd still be forced to compete.
That thought got me asking when I found
the mouth. Had my brother found it before me?
Was he still running? I waited by the mouth
for ages, wanting to shout for him and being afraid
to make a sound for the other bodies. I kept
one hand on the lip to reserve it, kept my other extended,
and right when I was willing to let myself be unfound,
the mouth opened, just enough for my arm to be taken.
The lips turned over me and themselves creating suction
for my body to come in, and though the lips were chapped,
and the skin splintered into sharp razors, I prayed for my sake,
and my brother's, that my pain wouldn't end before his.

Hell's Conditions

In Hell, all bodies are reduced. Flesh drops
from where it's been burned, and where it lands,
separates. Bones bleach after the blood makes a vapor
or stain, then everything regenerates just enough
to perpetuate the pain. The scent of death is constant
in the winds, even when Hell is airless. The smell works
up through nostrils to souls that process regardless.
Hell works because it imbues everything with loss
or losing. Something is always taken short
of the horizon. The journey never completes for being
forced to see the destination retreat. Even screams
are normalized. I hear them the same as the whirring
of air conditioning, my own breathing, provoking
commentary only in a particular threat or struggling.
I could always tell the bodies who'd been down longest
or were smart enough to beat the game. They were always
the ones off to the side sitting or standing like flagpoles,
silver hair thrashing as if to say, *If I were still going,
I'd be going that way.*

Dying Aspects

At some point, everyone I knew came to realize
we're dying much quicker than we thought we would.
We were as polite as we could be about it in conversation
over brews and breakfast, pollen breathed on clear days
and park benches. We never called it what it was,
always opting for its implications: food intolerances,
allergies, and aches. The pain in my thigh
seemed to appear overnight, but a creeping of years
had brought it on. When I tried, I couldn't name
the years my body was painless, but I thought the period
would last longer. In my sprint to worthiness,
I guess it's not unreasonable for some pain to come
in the third decade. I'd been working so hard
to enjoy this life. The needs of human beings
can be massive the way we've insisted on
meeting them. In Hell, time stopped working
against my brother and me. We'd never die,
so there was no rush, but there was also no need
to let go of the debate, who between the two of us
loved who most, who had more of God inside of him,
and who was the better child, as if the world were one
in which things didn't grow, as if you would be praised
for remaining a child in a world in which things did.
No death would bring about a regret worth forfeiting
these superlatives. No matter the pains, in Hell,
we'd both live through them.

A Forgetting Statement

My brother and I must've been bored
throwing the balloon beside our twin beds,
his against the far wall. Mine intended
for the other wall but with space on both sides
to fall off of it. Not saying much,
we must have been upset. *I'm still up*
for being brothers if you are, I said.
It's been ages. I don't remember how old
we were, but I must've also been desperate.
My brother gnarled his face in a way
I was used to, but in a way I'd run from
on a stranger coming toward me from darkness.
Just throw the balloon, he said. I kept
thinking it must not have been what he wanted.
Even now I can see the balloon. Its light
drifting back and forth, the brown arms a blur
behind it, the two-armed reaches, the throws,
the hands, the double palmed catches, even
the features on our young and goofy faces,
and the rest of the room swirling like clouds
on a hostile planet. Despite the decay,
the memory remains. It's because it remains
that I'm trusting it. Does the memory become
reality if you and your brother are still inside
when the world ends, if only one of you
ever comes out of it?

A Search Through Liquid Fire

I'd never traveled one mountain,
hill, or body of water
in search of my brother.

I've traveled caves and caverns
in Hell, liquid fire,
stretches of brown rock.

My brother and I were always close,
and being close, no one thought
to tell us the elusive things

we could search for
inside each other. Finding myself
on a cliff, I was amazed

overlooking the valley
hundreds of bodies
had found before me.

In the center of them
were two fiery funnel storms
swirling faster around

each other with each moment.
From the bottom up, each
serpentine weather washed

red to blue. Delirious, the bodies
in proximity ran toward them
to be sucked upward, hurled

through the skies. I think
they did it hoping that higher
it would be cooler, that

they'd be thrown to the world
above this one. No longer knowing
how far anyone had fallen,

there was no guarantee if it proved true
that the world they found
would be the one they left.

Maybe it didn't mean anything that Hell
was rarely flat and massive.
None of the bodies I saw travel

the storms fell downward. The longer
the storms danced and closer,
they, like my brother and I,

never merged. Their fire
morphed from a blue
more white than anything

to azure, and though the mutation
increased the heat in Hell dramatically,
everyone continued watching for the beauty.

Whirling

I swallowed a firestorm
walking through Hell. I'd spent
so much time
wandering the flames
my skull's sharp lines
protruded. My jaw
dislodged itself,
made an oval
at a slant
for that whirling
to work in.
The dark inside
writhed around it,
each sliver folded
in favor of that
violent light, then
I realized I hated
my brother had become
the thing to find,
that perhaps
the storm was one
I conjured
to survive his finding,
and that
if I ever found him,
ever allowed myself
one word
to that occasion,
that violence
might be all
I had left
to give him.

Beacon

The first time I made my brother cry with words
felt like a victory. I understood
he was human, but tears seemed
out of reach. I'd already
made him cry
by hitting him
with my hands
or heavy objects,
but I was always
the one crying
at the end
of his verbal volleys,
half because of what he said,
half because he did it
for amusement
or out of anger,
and being younger,
I was sure
I wouldn't find words
big or cutting enough
to hurt, even knowing
sometimes
I thought he was stupid.
He'd gained weight that year.
He started singing
socially. I knew
I could cut an opening
if lunged, if at once,
I attacked him
from both directions.
We were in front
of his friend
when he started crying.

What had I said? I thought,
how could he have let
his friend see that? Everyone
always expected him
to win, and I, having won,
having gotten past
the newness, wanted
to win again. How even
had we gotten following
that trend over the years?
At what point in the world
had we become
infected? The truth is,
dropped into
the middle of the ocean,
I'm sure we would both drown.
No one would blame us
for dying, for not being found,
for not being able
to save each other.
Same goes for being
trapped under a pile
of rubble, of burning black
in a blocked
and blazing building,
though it might be noted
if our bodies were found
huddled together, if the space
between us indicated
an insistence, to a painful end,
refusing to be separated.
Brother, haven't we done
the best we can over time
for knowing better?
Both wanting to live
we might've killed each other

for being dressed in armor
and wielding weapons
in a closed stadium,
fighting with all we had
convinced
only one of us could,
or cannibalizing the other
on some island
when the other died
from hunger
or at the start
of some sickness
for having no medicine.
I'd like to think
these days we'd just
throw our hands up,
knowing life is
the most wonderful
and not at all
worth fighting the other
to keep it.
Brother, we're not
close enough these days
to prove it to each other.
Tell me
we trust each other
enough
to risk it.

Lying Down

Every body that hits the ground in Hell
will get up should they choose it.
There's plenty of death and destruction
but no dead. All ends are artificial,
wishful thinking, and even running,
even seeing their soft resolve lie
face down, you feel sorry for them.
Some bodies are so far decided, and in
some areas their lying so dense. You try
your best not to step on them, but when
you do, most times they don't bother
to make a sound. They mimic
what they remember of the dead things
from when they lived. In the crowds
of the bodies still making their way,
I've found myself running over
the planks the lying make, stepping
on the backs of their charcoaled heads,
their heads inducing a misstep
as they sink, as I further bury
their faces. It's the stress of the flames
behind us that causes this, that encourages
our rapid, collective pacing. It's easy
to fall. One falling becomes many
and many makes a felled section,
but soon enough the disturbed tide
of running finds a balance,
and those of us who have gone under
it seems for hours are forced to be
the fodder of those whose timing is better.
I remember watching TV upstairs.
Upstairs, the entertainment center
held easily the biggest TV in the house,

only with the weight distributed as it was
with the TV inside, it was even easier
for everything to tumble over.
My brother half watched while he browsed
at the computer. My feet rested
on the lower half of the center,
not realizing its rocking as I pushed.
I'll admit I understood badly what it meant
to be mad at a person. I thought once
it happened, they withdrew from you.
You could no longer count on them,
and to make things even or protect yourself,
you'd also withdraw your protection.
My father taught me that. I remember
learning the lesson from my brother,
but also the day he complicated it.
The TV stand began to tip over.
Having realized right away,
I might've been able to escape,
but I merely fell and waited
to be crushed. My brother, with one arm,
pushed it back. I remember thinking,
why would you do that? Had you been
waiting for something bad to happen to me,
this was your chance. It would've made me
sad, but I would've given it to you.
Years back, when we were both tiny,
the same thing happened to him,
only no one was there to save him.
I can't remember if I watched it happen,
but I'd seen its aftermath, my brother
flailing under the weight of the thing,
and crying. I don't believe I would've
been strong enough to stop it,
but I don't trust the memory, or myself
inside of it, to know I would have

had I been, and I thank God for that.
I only need to atone for the present.
If the only world is a Hell with my brother
in it, being with him will make a new one.

Human Devices, Unsupervised

Everything in Hell is unsupervised.
I used to think there would be
sentinels in the form of beasts
or our fallen human likenesses
to mock us, keep us from breaking
locks on secret doors
and entering them,
and perhaps remind us
there could be an us
against them to keep sacred
what we all had in common,
but the lack of supervision
is more insidious
and lonely. Human devices,
once ugly, are those that can
progress infinitely.
The screams that let out
let out and fall back on us.
A body next to you becomes
a board shielding you
from scorching winds,
and though the board squirms
being used for that purpose,
and you can smell
its cooked and rotten bits
after it has burned,
you discard it with no difference.
When the air that's thick
with soot or ash
latches in some body's throat, provoking
a cough so violent it hemorrhages
but won't clear for becoming blood
vomit, everyone just watches

or doesn't but walks past, the mentality
being, like a cat hacking up,
it'll pass, it'll pass. There are regions
in Hell with plenty pain
and no screaming as if
people had forgotten the function,
as if any expression of what was felt
could be a trait bred out of humans,
but no, it doesn't take Hell
for that to happen. Before this,
there were all sorts of things
we humans would do to let
those around know the pain
we were in. Was it a hope
we had or some selfish survival
mechanism? Had it been us
inflicting the pain,
those shrill signals could scare
us into different behavior, but then,
even then, there were those
who would hear and continue
brutalizing. Supervised or not,
I remember always asking myself
what happened to them? How was it
they found Hell before we did,
and even showing it to us,
how could we not recognize
before we all slipped in?

The Breeze

It seems there have always been people
claiming time passes differently in Hell,
as if, from the beginning, there's been
a Hell to go to and a Hell
whose grasp you could break from.
Time has always been different
to my brother and me. Our trek
was supposed to be a dream,
benign, temporary, if hideous
and unflinching. I dreamt of my brother
before but never burning, never
screaming through everlasting fire.
Never in the dreams could he leave.
I wondered if the dream could be his, if
he could trick me into being the one
to finish it. He left me inside the house
for the outside, made fire
the only way to him. I could
feel myself changing under the heat,
but the way I saw it I'd never finish
burning. *Surely we could open the door,*
he said. *Surely there'll be a breeze.*
The temperatures inside were suffocating.
He was right. For all the wind on which
the flames carried, there was a breeze
we could enjoy if I could perform a dousing,
but why leave it to me? I wanted him to see
the fires I made up close. I wanted to tell him
I was sorry that was all I could offer before
he insisted on standing in the middle of them.

Hell Swallowed

One enters a Hellmouth like a snack but exits like a bullet. Crushed between its lips, the body becomes a beautiful, metallic, and oily object. Where the lips turn it over, they split. Blood rushes the body crimson and over the tongue as a pulpy liquid, bubbles acidic down the tongue's slope to a throat but no swallow, only a slap against a back, a wall of red flesh for blood to eat through. The body boils and reforms again, and when the longest time has passed, the wall opens. Blood splashes all around you, steams on a white surface and you realize the steam is a gift. Beyond the mouth, Hell turns to ice. You can walk awhile feeling almost nothing, a temperature you think might be normal before your limbs stiffen, before they swell and blacken. Your body becomes a block, useless to you, but it phases, and between phasing, you can think. You think about all the invisible things a body carries inside a mind and you think, if you could just cut them out, sever them from the body and yourself, there'd be nowhere left for Hell to find you.

Sasquatch

I trekked barefoot in a land of endless sheets of ice,
marveling at the blueness overhead,
underneath, my thoughts separating with the cracks
in its surface, their sharpness, the cold cuts made

of my falling feet. I felt the skin of my heels split
wide openings for the land's sharp objects, their lodging,
as if thirsty, a thirst relieved with their soft melting
and the leaked blood behind me.

Imperfect as the prayer was, I prayed for an end
to myself. Not knowing the fool
that prayer would leave. Each pulled breath heavy,
each hand outstretched to a sun no warmer

for its blinding. The skin on my arms tears
against the rush of the wind, the cold's cruel breach
of my bones with the day's retreat into night,
my skull's buckling, my rattling jaw,

and my organs made stones to roll inside an abdomen
I'd continue to carry all the same. Is this the kind of extreme
that teaches us all pain is transformation,
and our preference for pain that's knowing or brainless?

Could that lesson be the one all cold deaths leave?
Could it be that's how thoughts remain after the body,
and that each step taken in this land
becomes one by which I won't go missing?

Prayers and Preservation

The cold in Hell whirls
so tightly around the body,
forms a grip so painful,
it takes everything
to keep moving.
Its entire crystal presence is ice.
Its only expression is ice,
shards and flecks and hurls of ice,
and where mountains
and grounds might've been
are only junctures
forever deep of ice.
You walk slow to preserve the body.
You walk fast to preserve the mind,
and then, as if finally in sync, the two of you
stop caring. You betray each other.
The two of you march forward
despite the other's breaking.
I remember reaching the point
the cold's weight was so heavy
that my legs sank into the ice.
Its crystals wedged
between the cells of my skin
and where it split was frozen.
I could see on the limbs
a glittering, a rich tapestry
of rubies and diamonds.
The skin was so brittle
what didn't crush or crumble
would tear, and though I could feel it tearing
I stretched my arms higher in the air,
triumphant, because I was still moving.
I lifted them not knowing they would break

and when they fell, and where,
I wouldn't look at them.
I kept walking until my legs were broken,
until I'd fallen flat
on my face. I had determination
and nothing to keep me.
All my shreds turned to waste,
and I lay on the ice for so long,
and I prayed for everything in it
to cave, to take me,
and when I'd forgotten the prayers,
the ice broke, and from under
the crumbling came a black liquid
I shook my head through to be sure,
and it washed over what was left
and it washed over what I'd lost
and took us to the ocean. For all
the rumors of Hell's water, all
that vain, thirstful searching
I thought, finally,
I found it.

Another Bed in Hell's Ocean

You first find Hell's ocean on the seabed,
two feet planted on its bubbling and grainy surfaces.
Perhaps if one could glimpse the waters
from the horizon, no one would jump in,
thirst quenched.

All bodies on the bed drift upward,
a grace to those who are too tired
to fight its currents, those
who can't swim until they learn
the dark waters are chiefly acid, and the lift
too slow for a burn so wet and constant.

Most often the bubbles collect a crown
around my mouth, a ring of barnacles that bite.
The sores they leave are bloody but under a violence
too turbulent to get infected, but then
there are times the bubbles work a way up
and through the entire skin of my face,
a gentle abrasive burning
from chin to forehead.

The skin takes and ejects into the ocean.
When it's pulled away from me
I see myself in a way no mirror could let me
before the waters destroy the image.

Though I roam Hell in search of my brother,
I can only find myself. So many times my face has
let loose in this ocean. I used to think
the parts I left behind would leave me
the thinnest of what I was. I see now
that what's left is most potent,

thickest, the shapes of which
I work hardest to determine if they make me
sick or the proudest I've ever been, but is it
for this question I've had my brother traded?
If I loved him, I never said it, and if I never found him
I wouldn't need to be afraid.

In Hell's Ocean I Come upon a Man Wanting His Sons' Approval

And though I'm only one,
I know the man in the corner is
my father, even as
his body is tucked in sand.
His skin, gelatinous,
with blue rings that glow
on several limbs.
When he stirs the limbs,
black grains
curl around them.
I'd never unknow that face
and the look on it.
He lies as big as God
in the minds of believers,
but when he stands
he stands a man that fits
in the palm of my hand,
so I lift him. His limbs
glide through the water,
its near-invisible music,
as a dancer's. When I begin
to swing my head, he copies
the movement, and when I stop,
he stops as if discouraged,
so I start again.
I encourage him.
I raise him to be strong
and confident, with confidence
he'd never give.
His worn face turns
young again
and over seconds,

his head and body age
old again, and I see.
His Hell is a magic
I break by forgiving him,
and I forgive him
so he'll die
being the man
he just learned
he always wanted to be,
and when it's done,
he shatters. His shards
crumble a dust
of blue shimmers,
and he releases,
leaves wounded
and clever sons
with still-burning flames
inside them, undoused
by Hell's darkest hold
in its only ocean,
and unfathered,
with no children
to find or be found by,
but at least knowing
Hell is a place
you walk in
after you cut
the heart open.

At Some Point, Light Lets Through

After a while floating through Hell's waters,
enough light lets through
for you to see other bodies
floating inevitably upward
and disintegrating. So long
as you keep a distance, the acidic
waters make beauty of us.
Millions of fizzing bubbles
lift from our bodies' slow burning
and glimmer. We turn with
the currents, sometimes making
angelic movements,
our clothes orbit wraith-like ruin
around us, and the ocean
makes wild spreads of our long locks
of hair. The viewing itself
is magical. The acid
clouds and fades the image
in our eyes, then between
burning them to complete darkness,
returns the image, briefly,
with the sharpest resolution.
This realm of Hell is one in which
it's most true what happens
to one happens to everybody.
At some point on the way up,
something changes.
The water clogs with bodies.
I remember I once floated
closer and closer to another one,
a lady I guessed was my age.
At one point between our tossing,
close floating, our eyes met,

and though the image was cloudy
we reached to each other
until our hands met,
and though we were both burning,
and this close the beauty
I described had long left, we smiled
and held on past when our hands
became bones and raw flesh again,
until the drift broke
us apart. I remember after
we separated, I had so many questions
for her, who she was,
the person looking for her,
the person she was searching for.
Of all the bodies I could've
washed into, the two of us
decided to make a pair
with smiles we fought hard
to retain and remember,
that holding on to her hand,
that moment. I'll never
see her again.

IV

Fossil Fuel

Moments after Hell's ocean allows you to reach its surface,
the world turns over. You dart through the boiling waters
like a rocket straight into one of its geysers.
It gropes you. It coats you in waste as inside a bowel,
but once fully committed, it's you who becomes
the movement. The journey is dark so your mind illuminates.
All those bodies floating at the top of the water and not one
of them moving. You tilt your head downward, but there's
nothing to see, no chest, feet, and so you remind yourself
they're still parts of your body, and the sky is red or pink
or maybe pink and red with no stars, and then everything flips,
as though the sky could fill, as if this part of Hell
were a cylinder filled with liquid filled with rocks and sand
and living ornaments some giant child could turn over
for amusement, and you fall or you float or you fall and float
headfirst into another world you can't escape. You surface
in a place that looks like the world you left or one adjacent
where you can manage, where you did manage. Out of the geyser
you rise like a man pulled from quicksand. You clear the mud
from your eyes. The sun blinds but then you see. This world
is one of vast greens in sharp shapes attached to brown trunks
and vines. You wipe the mud from your limbs and when
you've cleared them, you wish you hadn't because the flies
that attach to them bite, and where they bite the blood runs
and from where it runs mites burrow, and within the burrows
you're compelled to scratch and where you scratch the burrows
widen and from the widening the blood pours and in the pour
the dead mites. You feel faint, but you realize you've walked a ways
from where you started. The loss is overwhelming, but ahead
of you, there are tracks. You want to fall but think not again,
and you think: no matter the man the tracks belong to,
you must find him.

An Overgrowth Besides the Body

Hell's jungle is an overgrowth of green.
The leaves that jut from the ferns, fall
down from the trees, do so with such sharpness
you cut yourself with any brush by them.
Every movement you make is one
made through a grater. You leave
so much of yourself behind
under the wetness and burning.
The sun's rays and humidity
make your droppings sizzle
on some surfaces. The smell
they release in this sector is appetizing,
or would be, if you weren't also wilting
under the steamy beams. You walk
each path with a drooping,
the question mark of your body
forever-curling into a gnarl
of lost meaning. The wounds you host
fester. The fungus builds an island
of moss on your neck, center-back,
and shoulders, amass a mail
on your chest and lower body,
and under the moss
is pus you can drain if you squeeze
or scratch too deep.
Beyond the pus is the blood
you've known so well already,
but even so, sometimes,
it rains. The conditions resting
on the grounds rise. The clouds
work up into big gray billows
and the whole of the jungle
darkens. The shadows

are everywhere, falling
astral straw under the foliage
before dissolving
completely, and then
the flash shows. Lightning
then thunder as we've
always perceived it,
then more of both. The rain
falls violently on the greens
but tempers a bit making
its way through the density.
The jungle cools.
The water washes you
before it floods the venue
and rises into the trees.
You hitch a ride floating
on top of it. The leaves on the branches
don't cut when they're wet.
They soften and bend,
and so you sit on them.
You wait out the flooding
on the tree branches, climbing
higher with the water.
You stop when it peaks.
Way high up in the canopy,
you see everything
besides another body.

In Hell's Jungle, a Knock to No Eye

After the flooding,
the jungle's sediments
swirl inside each other,
create a marbling
on the floor. Somehow,
the floodwaters
grow giant,
monstrous flowers
that don't open
immediately after
the water is absorbed.
While they're closed,
they glow a green
more brilliant
than emeralds,
but when they bloom,
the petals show pale
as new flesh, release
a scent as rancid
as dead men's mouths,
but every now
and then, a clear liquid
starts to pour
from them. They form
a jelly bed
over the ground's
sharp objects
before their stigmas
birth whole bodies.
Each takes the shape
of my brother's.
Where they fall
on the jelly, my brother

writhes, but each one
brought to term
has already died.
Each time I rush
to them. I try
to beat life
into my brother
so we can make off,
leave Hell together.
I knock so hard
on the chests
they crush,
and though
over a long span
of time I crush
them to a death,
I know they crush
to spite me.
Not even Hell
can help me yield
my brother's harvest.
For all the bodies
I found and all
the knocking,
there wasn't one
I could hit hard enough
to open his eyes.

My Brother's Two Screams

I heard two screams from my bedroom. Outside,
my brother had killed his best friend. That day
the clouds stayed put. The trees swayed under
gentle winds, but not enough to disturb the birds,
and the sun shined so brightly on the cars. I remember
thinking it's rare that passion and proximity correlate
so strongly. My brother and I lived so close for so long
in the house, but the passion we had for each other came
in waves, cooled to familiarity that remained even if
it dulled when we both left the house. Each day
we spent in each other's presence after that was
a discovery, not quite on edge but never without one.
We tiptoed up to remembering what we forgot
we'd always know about the other, calling each other
the names no one in our adult lives knew,
but not knowing what to say having used them.
Would you eat a salad if I fixed one? Is that how you eat?
My brother killed his best friend with a word
I couldn't hear. He fell slowly into the street.
When his body hit the concrete, it burst into
a tidal wave, the broth of which split in two and rushed
in opposite directions. The asphalt drank my brother's
friend through cracks it made on its surface.
I stayed outside watching, thinking they would close
when my brother's friend had gone completely,
but vines crept through and kept them open.
They spiraled as high as my knees, bloomed blue
and red-orange flowers, and I thought, at least
he got it easier, at least he could go on being all the things
one can be in this life when they're no longer a friend
to my brother. My brother's words couldn't kill me.
Sometimes I wonder if it's my fault he doesn't
share words with me before knowing better. Perhaps
there aren't any. I guess I should be grateful.

A Difference

I wish I could explain the danger that lies in a look
through a window. People will say, *Why not
draw the shades? It's a beautiful day outside.*
Having seen, I'll agree, but left alone with the view,
the beauty tugs so strongly on my eye that
the vessels inside it break, and so the beauty bleeds.
The sky stirs. Red leaks into the blue. The sky turns
purple marvelously, but the red keeps leaking until
there is only red, a red so rich so high in the sky,
and the wind blows. All the trees lose their greens.
The waters wash over the grounds, and then in the sky,
there's lightning. It strikes in straight lines then arcs
and branches, then the branches become limbs
that swirl everything together. The window
I look through and the room I'm sitting in are fine,
and at some point, the world interrupts. This time
it's my brother. I recognize his knock even if
it's different. When I open the door, his hand
is a fist hanging away from his arm and himself
like a bird feeder, wrapped and bound by a loose
stretch of skin. It seems to swing a bit and twist as if
someone were giving it a gentle spin. It occurs to me
my brother used it to get my attention. He wanted me
to see. Had he experienced the day like I had, only
to this difference? His room was just up the stairs.
By the light up there, he'd also drawn the shades
and stared in. His wrist was broken, but he'd gotten
both of us away from it. He hadn't said anything
and wouldn't answer, even as I popped him in place,
even as I wrapped the bandages around him.

Things I've Thought, Things I Do

My brother used to say it would only take a punch to put me in the hospital. Long before he made telling me a habit, when the piles of muscle he grew into mountains stretched trenches in his skin, I knew.

◎

Taunted with the inevitable that long, I ran, over and over, straight toward it. I couldn't be powerless if I made him do it.

◎

I'd rush him. He'd wrap his arms around my arms, lift me into the air and set me back down again. It went like this, so many episodes of his waiting for me to finish, not realizing I ran toward him wanting, then waiting, for him to finish me.

◎

All those times I pictured myself in a bed under sterile lighting hooked up and comatose or dead. We had no idea we were getting exactly what we wanted for how different the picture rendered in our heads.

◎

I could never take my brother at his word. I'd put so much faith in words. I thought the thing about the hospital meant that's what he wanted, so I was happy to leave him. I pretended I didn't mind the method.

◎

Brother, why did you insist so much on saying it? Even when it was obvious that wasn't what you wanted; I think it took so long to sink in because I couldn't answer that question.

◎

How many laughs had I missed out on all those times being lifted into the air? The air rushing up and again, my legs kicking like on rides I was so excited about, standing hours in line through summer heat at the theme parks.

◎

Brother, who could've told us the fun we were having? These days when I sift through the past like this, when you're lying next to me on the bed before you're lost again, I'm trying to tell you what I will miss.

A Scheme

My brother and I used to scheme
to make money. It was our way
of coping with the tiny allowances
our father gave us, a coping
he didn't realize would make us
creative, my brother less so
because his allowance was always
double mine. Those days
were adjacent to digging for treasure
in our backyard, of looking into
a blue sky and dreaming of being
sailors discovering large chests
of jewels under the ocean.
The world had so many limits
back then, imposed by a man
who became a dad so the grudge
he held against his family
would pay attention to him,
but even looking at the perimeter,
the ordinary, localized possibilities
of a house whose backyard
was marked by a boundary
of gray wood, we became masters
of projection. We never sold
lemonade in the street. It was what
the other kids in the neighborhood
and the kids on TV were doing,
but perhaps they were happy,
perhaps they didn't know selling
sweetened citrus in a Dixie cup
full of vital liquid for a quarter
or 50 cents was no amount of money

that could take them anywhere, perhaps
under their houses wasn't a fire
whose fingers curled around them.

In the Center of Hell's Jungle Is a Massive Tree

Finding it, I sensed
I was staring at a human
being, a human
that had wandered
to the heart,
lifted its arms,
and rooted itself
to stay, its head
extending upward
indefinitely. There
was no way around the tree,
its trunk standing a barrel
that would unravel for miles,
a trunk pushing so tightly
against the surrounding foliage
as to make baleen, starving
any whale it meant to
filter feed. I'd given my brother
so much of my energy
creating Hell with such
marvelous, living features,
and for so long I didn't
realize how much
I was exhausting.
I put my ear on the bark
as though my hearing
could stretch
an infinite reach.
I felt my brother
was on the other side,
but I didn't know how to get
to him. I cut at the tree,
and from every cut,

sap black as blood
leaked. Boiling, it fell
to the ground and where
it fell on the ground kept
bubbling. The cuts I made
specked blood on the bark
and blood on the leaves.
The bark would sizzle
and the leaves would wilt
and fall so bloody,
but there wasn't a cut
I could make deep enough
to dissolve the tree,
so I embraced it,
its already widely
outstretched arms
newly barren,
and though the limbs
cracked and curled
inward to embrace me,
I couldn't feel anything,
and though embraced
with the cuts I'd made
all around me,
I couldn't make it
mean anything.

Still a Loss

Of course there are others in the world I could call brother.
It's just I can't move past seeing them as failures
after losing you, after the run of blood in our veins,
the lineage, the different expressions of it on our skin and faces,
and the house in which, for so many years, we shared it.
You told me to *get over it*. That you already were,
but you were a liar or would be if I was sure you knew
what the truth was. Somehow, every one of my brothers
outside of the house knows more about me than you do now,
but I wonder if those untapped sources inside you mean
you would always know me better. Outside of the house,
I try to make the best bonds of what's happened to me.
I never told you I knew what it felt like
to have my body spread from the back, have it slapped
back together in a room with dim lighting by someone
who never promised I'd enjoy it but scare me just enough
to let him do it over and over, that even though
you were years older, I maybe could've told you
years before it would cross your mind that
any invasion on the body, or inside of it, feels
like an abuse, but it's better if it's something you choose.
I could've maybe told you if you ever lost your ability
to choose, you could lose yourself, that your mind could catch fire
over the wild things one does to get it back, but only
to learn again, if invasion is one of the things enacted,
that it will always feel abusive no matter who you do it with.
I would sit with you, say it sucked. You'd struggle to make sense
of me saying I don't understand how a person could fuck
someone they claim to love. I tried to make a brother
out of someone who already knew those things, who had already
been invaded. I thought the world of him. We read about invasion
in each other's writing. We hardly talked about it.
That silence was comforting at first, before I learned silence

could never measure the amount of thinking done on the subject,
the kind. He'd been drinking, but his line of thinking
must've preceded his sluggish utterance of it at the bar.
I told him he'd been wrong about how he thought
I'd been coping, said I only know about men through the grudge
I hold with them. I wouldn't take it further short of feeling safe,
but I hope to, if only for a little while. I know it's unfair
to ask somebody to be one thing forever. *Yeah,* he said,
because if you pursued them, you'd be accepting
the fate of your abuser. And I thought, well, before,
when he thought I had, did he pity me, did he think of me
with a disgust that made him feel guilty? I was reminded
of all those who say of us who've had our choice removed
that those who have sex with the sex of their abuser do so
because they enjoyed their abuse. I think I realized my brother
had made the mistake of believing everyone around him
who'd never been through what we had. Those people
could've killed him. I think I was the one person who refused,
who knew accepting the fate of an abuser means doing
what they did even knowing the damage, that what you've lost
will still be lost when the whole world loses it.

V

Souls Side by Side

My brother and I
had souls
to swirl
vast darkness.
To that debt,
we gave our dad
everything,
his hands locked
around our faces
until he left.
He's come back
to two men
who can only move
to knife the other
who can only reach
to cleave.
He creeps
around us
pining
like he hadn't died
when he first left.
Father, why
are you dying?
We killed you.
You should be dead.

Hell's Wide Net

I cast a wide net in Hell for my brother.
I was both the person who held the net
and the bait inside, my arms craning
back and throwing forward, letting
the string reel through my hands,
and holding it against the current
when it landed. The Hell he swam in
and his swimming and my pouring in
a kind of nourishment, and that,
whether good or bad. In the past,
the ambiguity had done the trick.
I told myself the difference Hell made
was that this time, make or burn,
it would be the same to both of us.
I'd hoped to lure my brother in
knowing I wasn't what he wanted
while knowing I was all I had
toward that purpose. He wouldn't
want Hell more. I wouldn't have
to trap him as much as bring him home.
I was always afraid when we were little,
wanting to go where he went but still
afraid to pursue the violence, being told
not to follow him. That trained-in anxiety
never left me in my older age, in Hell.
I couldn't be abandoned for never being
with him. He taught me there's so much else
in the world to be with. I don't think
he understood. I followed him so closely
back then because the world was one
I didn't recognize when I couldn't see him.

Murky Water

There's a rush I get
fishing in murky waters.
What lives inside them
can't easily be seen.
I'm unnerved being brought
into proximity
with the other senses
that let me know
I've found something.
It's horrifying
when the body
I've managed
to snag on the hook
is heavy, and as I pull it
toward the surface,
I absorb its violent lashes
on the line, the hook
through its body
an imposition,
letting loose a vital flare
through the waters
in a loosening red streak
as the creature phases
vaguely between several
shapes and colors. I think
for a moment
there's a possibility
what I've caught
is a monster the world has
never seen. I've seen
the surface of Hell's ocean.
I've passed through

its waters. There is no coast
to sit on, on which
to receive anything.
I'm the only one
who's ever come fishing,
and though there are millions
of bodies in Hell's waters,
and none of them are biting
for not being hungry, I've only
come for my brother. I hope
he'll find me, that he
won't leave me waiting,
but then again, I'm nervous.
I hope his pulling on the line
is something I recognize,
that the brutality of the waters
could leave room
for the possibility
he'll be happy to see me.
The waters in Hell are burning,
and so too will my brother
when he comes. From where
he comes, his flesh
will have eroded. His flesh
will be wet and exploding,
and perhaps his eyes will be cloudy,
and if he has the power of speech,
there's no telling he'll use it,
and if he uses, there's no guarantee
what he'll say, so while I wait
in his pulling to the surface,
I pray the sight of him won't change
my thinking. I want to be brave,
to bring him in, but there's no telling

what in the distance has happened.
I pray somehow on his way up,
I don't drop him back in.

VI

The World at Its Beginning

I suppose every Hell is one
the Earth has already enacted.
We're told
little of the Earth
was unfrozen
during the Ice Ages,
that the world's origins
were molten,
those swirling flames
still deep below the surface
and at the core,
that the bacteria
crowning the round runs
of the vents
shooting water and sulfur up
from the sea floor
most resemble
the organisms that rose
the world's
flesh endowed
life forms,
and that the first
of the world's green lands
had a wildness of abundance
we humans cut back
over hundreds of years
to make us comfortable,
to give us a culture
we'd come to document
at least as much
as we lived.
There wasn't a time
I didn't have

a brother. When
my eyes opened,
he was already here.
But there's so little
time between us,
he also can't remember
a time before me.
Our origins blur
into a single birth
between us
and so between us
is a world
and its beginning.
I tell myself
there's not a world
without my brother in it.
I tell myself
I'd follow him anywhere
to keep the world
from ending.

Acknowledgments

32 poems: "The Breeze," "Dying Aspects";

The Account: "Fossil Fuel," "An Overgrowth Besides the Body";

Bennington Review: "In Hell's Ocean I Come upon a Man Wanting His Sons' Approval";

The Boiler: "A Difference," "A Scheme," "Souls Side by Side";

The Cortland Review: "A Forgetting Statement";

Fjords Review: "A Season in Hell with Rimbaud";

Flypaper Lit: "My Brother Outside the House in Hell";

Hobart: "Hell's Wide Net," "My Brother's Two Screams," "The World at Its Beginning";

Honey Literary: "Hell Swallowed";

The Literary Review: "A Dependency";

The Nation: "Lying Down";

Ovenbird: "Whirling";

PANK: "Another Bed in Hell's Ocean," "At Some Point, Light Lets Through";

Poetry Northwest: "Pain on a Soft Surface," "Watching My Brother Sleep in Hell, a Memory Reminds Me This Too Is Bonding";

Pushcart Prize XLV: "A Season in Hell with Rimbaud";

Split Lip Magazine: "In the Center of Hell's Jungle Is a Massive Tree," "In Hell's Jungle, a Knock to No Eye."

Thanks to Peter Conners and everyone at BOA Editions for making *A Season in Hell with Rimbaud* a BOA book and for making me a BOA poet. I'm so happy. Thanks to Nathan Mullins for projecting this dream with your hands and he(art).

Thanks to Norman Dubie. I think you saw this book's final form when I was convinced it was one poem first bringing it to you those years ago. Thanks to the Anderson Center at Tower View for the residency and for being the place I first finished this book. Thanks to Cathy Linh Che, Abbey Blake, Colwill Brown, and Rachael Kilgour for being my Anderson Center family and for supporting me and this book with everything you have and are. Thanks to Jenny Xu for the early affirmation and kind advice. Thanks to Michael Morse for "A Dependency." Thanks to Michael Shewmaker, Sebastián Hasani Páramo, K. Iver, and William Fargason for being supportive first readers and loving friends.

Thanks to Emily Jungmin Yoon, Raymond Antrobus, Paul Tran, Michael Torres, Kaveh Akbar, Ravi Howard, Nicholas Goodly, Glenn Shaheen, Jessica Lanay, Steve Castro, Christopher Citro, Paige Lewis, Maya Marshall, Bojan Louis, Aram Mrjoian, Josh Bell, Rita Mookerjee, Brandon Rushton, Malcolm Tariq, Allen Drexel, Noor Najam, Alexander Chee, L. Lamar Wilson, Jennifer Bartell, James Kimbrell, Sanderia Faye, Ben Mirov, Yolanda Franklin, Sally Ball, Joshua Aiken, Cynthia Hogue, Candace Wiley, Justin Phillip Reed, Phil Grech, Dexter Booth, Jillian Weise, Gia Shakur, Monifa Lemons, Daniel Ruiz, Christopher Rose, DaMaris Hill, Brionne Janae, and Robert Stilling. Your love and kindness help me do this longer. Thanks to Cave Canem, The Watering Hole, The Bread Loaf Writers' Conference, and all the beautiful and generous people I met there.

Thanks to my family. Thanks to God.

About the Author

Dustin Pearson is the author of two previous collections of poetry: *Millennial Roost* and *A Family Is a House*. In 2019, *The Root* named Dustin one of nine black poets working in "academic, cultural and government institutions committed to elevating and preserving the poetry artform." In 2020, a film adaptation of his poem "The Flame in Mother's Mouth" won Best Collaboration at the Cadence Video Poetry Festival. His writing has been recognized and featured by Shonda Rhimes and further distinguished by the Katherine C. Turner and John Mackay Shaw Academy of American Poets Awards, a 2021 Pushcart Prize, and fellowships from Cave Canem, the Bread Loaf Writers' Conference, The Watering Hole, The Virginia G. Piper Center for Creative Writing, and The Anderson Center at Tower View. He teaches creative writing at the University of Tulsa.

BOA Editions, Ltd. American Poets Continuum Series

Colophon

BOA Editions, Ltd., a not-for-profit publisher of poetry and other literary works, fosters readership and appreciation of contemporary literature. By identifying, cultivating, and publishing both new and established poets and selecting authors of unique literary talent, BOA brings high-quality literature to the public.

Support for this effort comes from the sale of its publications, grant funding, and private donations.

The publication of this book is made possible, in part, by the special support of the following individuals:

Anonymous
Bernadette Catalana
Christopher C. Dahl, *in memory of J. D. McClatchy*
James Long Hale
Margaret Heminway
Sandi Henschel
Nora A. Jones
Paul LaFerriere & Dorrie Parini
Jack & Gail Langerak
John & Barbara Lovenheim
Joe McElveney
Dan Meyers, *in honor of J. Shepard Skiff*
Boo Poulin
Deborah Ronnen
William Waddell & Linda Rubel
Michael Waters & Mihaela Moscaliuc
Craig Morgan Teicher